HAYNES EXPLAINS
GERMANS

Owners' Workshop Manual

© Haynes Publishing • Written by **Boris Starling**

Published in September 2017

A catalogue record for this book is available from the British Library

ISBN 978 1 78521 155 3

Haynes Publishing, Sparkford, Yeovil,
Somerset BA22 7JJ, UK
Tel: +44 (0) 1963 440635
Website: www.haynes.com

Haynes North America, Inc.,
861 Lawrence Drive, Newbury Park,
California 91320, USA

Printed and bound in Malaysia

Cover image from Getty Images

Illustrations taken from the
Haynes VW Super Beetle
Owners Workshop Manual

Written by **B**
Edited by **L**
Designed by

526 612 36 5

Safety first!

Are you kidding? These are the Germans we're talking about. Safety's their middle name. They conduct a full risk assessment before leaving their front door and another one before getting in the car. No German is happier than wearing personal protective equipment including but not limited to a hi-vis tabard, a hard hat, safety eyewear and steel-tipped boots. A little excessive for a trip to the shops? You may think so. I couldn't possibly comment.

Working facilities

Every last aspect in accordance with regulations, directives and Declarations of Conformity. Workplace temperature to be exactly 18.6°C to ensure optimum alertness and no falling asleep after lunch when you've had one stein too many, mentioning no names, Karl-Heinz. Radiant temperature, humidity and air velocity to fall within nationally recognised parameters as set out in Article 16 (1) of Directive 89/391/ JUTK/5JD/7658. Guards, interlocks, two-hand controls, light guards and pressure-sensitive mats to be fitted to all machinery. Including the toaster in the works kitchen.

Contents

Introduction

Once upon a time there was a young German boy named Rolf, and from the moment he was born he never said a word. In every other respect he was perfectly normal: he crawled and stood, walked and ran, jumped and climbed, smiled and played. He just never spoke. His parents took him to endless doctors, but none of them found anything wrong with him.

Then one day at lunch, not long before his eighth birthday, Rolf suddenly said: 'this soup is cold.'

His parents were amazed! 'Rolf!' they cried. 'You can speak!'

'Of course I can speak.'

'Then why haven't you said a single word before today?'

'Up until now,' Rolf said, 'everything has been entirely satisfactory.'

About this manual

The aim of this manual is to help you get the best value from the German. It can do this in several ways. It can help you (a) decide what work must be done (b) tackle this work yourself, though you may choose to have much of it performed by external contractors such as all those Greeks whose ferocious work ethic, commitment to paying taxes and not retiring on a full public-sector pension at the age of 53 met with such a rapturous welcome in Germany.

The manual has drawings and descriptions to show the function and layout of the various components. Tasks are described in a logical order so that even a novice can do the work. Not that he or she will get much of a chance, because at every stage there'll probably be a bloke from Wuppertal or Lippstadt dressed in immaculate stay-pressed action slacks and a golf jumper standing with his hands behind his back and saying 'may I suggest zat you do it zis vay? My vay? Zat is for ze best, ja? I vill just do zis bit. And maybe zis bit. And vun more just here – oh! All done.'

Dimensions, weights and capacities

Overall height

Men .... 1.81m, average. Would be 1.82m
.... if Jens would just wear his Cuban heels.
Women .... 1.65m, average. Can rise to 1.93m
.... when standing on their disapproval.
Longest Leberkäse (liver cheese) ..... 161.5m. Measured by a qualified
.... surveyor, of course. Opposed by vegans.

Overall weight

Average man .... 82.4kg. Or 92.4kg if measured directly
.... after Oktoberfest.
Average woman .... 67.5kg. Has permanent option of shifting
.... unsightly lard by getting rid of husband.

Consumption

Beer... 6 litres per person per day. Lightweights.
Bread and bratwurst .... 30kg per household per week (when dieting).
Frivolous household items .... 0. This is no laughing matter.

Engine

Stroke .... the white cat, Blofeld-style, while
.... emphatically not plotting world domination.
Power .... Germany has it all. Sometimes they let the
.... French have a little for a day or so.
Torque .... more a monologue, really. Someone telling
.... you what to do. That's the German way.
Bore .... Ja ja, Fritz, we all know that the E-class was
.... the high water mark of build quality and that
.... yours has done more kilometres than the
.... International Space Station.
Redline .... at you, if you drive too close to them.

Model characteristics

There are several characteristics which distinguish the German.

Order

Ah. There is nothing – not bratwurst, not mullet hairstyles, not even beating England on penalties – that the Germans love more than order. Their favourite phrase is 'alles in Ordnung', everything in order.

Ordnung is not just 'order'; it is tidiness, properness, appropriateness, correctness. It's the state of mind where everything not expressly permitted is forbidden ('verboten' is a word you hear a lot in Germany).

Every aspect of German life is ordered. Apartment blocks have the Hausordnung, train stations the Bahnhofsordnung, public swimming baths the Badeordnung. Even garden gnomes are subject to their own ordnung, the Gartenzwergordnung, which specifies that they may not be taller than 69cm and must have the following items:

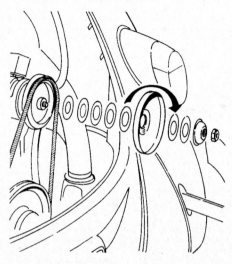

FIG 8•1 **THE QUICK BLACK ARROW JUMPS OVER THE LAZY CIRCLE**

a) beard
b) red cap
c) leather apron
d) spade over his shoulder
e) pickaxe
f) lantern
g) wheelbarrow

When in a fit of frankly treasonable unGermanness some allotment owners began to introduce non-standard gnomes – ones exposing their buttocks, making rude gestures or, worst of all, being girl gnomes – the authorities decided to act quickly and decisively. Did they launch night-time raids on the offending allotments? Publicly shame the non-compliant gnome owners?

No. Their solution was simpler. They declared that non-standard gnomes were not to be designated as gnomes at all. Order was therefore restored.

Punctuality

A close cousin of order. The Germans say 'punctuality is the politeness of kings' (conveniently forgetting they got rid of their own monarchy in 1918, though of course if they want to see a German royal family they can always come to Buckingham Palace).

You could set not just your watch but the atomic clock by a German's devotion to punctuality. If you invite them to a party at 7 p.m., they'll turn up at 6.50, walk round the block once for form's sake, and then ring your bell at precisely 6.55. You, expecting no-one to arrive until at least 7.30, will still be in the shower.

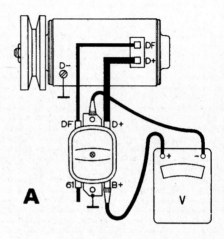

FIG 8·2 **A GERMAN'S WATCH IS CONNECTED TO HIS BRAIN AT ONE END...**

There are two concepts which may be common currency in most of the world but which the Germans simply and genuinely do not get:

i) fashionably late. There is 'on time' and there is 'late'. Neither have the slightest thing to do with fashion. 'On time' is normal and 'late' is rude.
ii) 'ish.' Saying 'be there around 8-ish' brings the Germans out in hives. This laxness, this elasticity, this choice: these cannot be permitted.

In defence of their position, the Germans point out that there are no movies called Quarter Past High Noon, The 3.10 To Yuma Is Running Late And We Apologise For The Inconvenience, or Nine Thirty To Five.

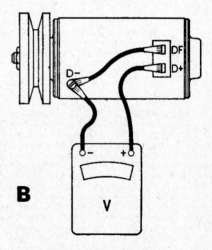

FIG 8·3 **... AND TO THE ATOMIC CLOCK AT THE OTHER**

Added extras

1. Stubbornness

The German changes direction so slowly and reluctantly that a supertanker looks like a BMX bike in comparison. Once a German holds an opinion, it is almost impossible to shift him away from it. Even if by some miracle you do manage to change his mind, don't expect him to acknowledge it. He will explain away any subsequent alteration of behaviour as 'the way it's always been', which brings us neatly onto...

NAH MATE. IT'S NOT EVEN BUDGING AN INCH

FIG 8•4 **ATTEMPTING TO GET A GERMAN TO CHANGE HIS MIND**

2. Bluntness

The Germans tell you what they think and they tell you straight. There's a thin line between being blunt and being rude, and this line gets crossed quite often without the Germans particularly caring. If you ask them whether your bum looks big in this and they tell you that it does – well, then it must. If you didn't want the answer then you shouldn't have asked the question.

Ask the Germans how they are and they'll tell you. Try and make small talk and they'll give you the kind of look Medusa spent an hour a day practising in the mirror. The British say no when they mean yes, the Americans yes when they mean no, and the French just shrug. The Germans say yes for yes and no for no.

If the strength of their handshakes is anything to go by, they also clearly have titanium metacarpals.

If it's true that whenever two Brits are together they'll form a queue, so too do three Germans together make a club.

3. Traditions

Germans love their traditions: not just the big ones such as Oktoberfest, Christmas and winning World Cups, but the smaller ones too. The Germans go on holiday to the same place at the same time of year for decades on end. They drive not just one make of car but one model within that make, which they replace at exactly three-yearly intervals having done exactly the same number of kilometres each year. They use the same plumber or electrician until one of them dies (hopefully not through flooding or electric shock). Basically, it's OCD on a national scale.

4. Education

The Germans are a well-educated and cultured bunch. It is not uncommon to find people well into their 30s on their third or fourth university degree. And yes, if someone has two separate doctorates, you should call them 'Doctor Doctor.' You should not follow this up with either a joke ('Doctor doctor, I've got wind/Good, here's a kite') or a reference to the 1984 song of the same name by the Thompson Twins, not least because, as every German knows, the Thompson Twins from the Tintin books weren't twins. In fact, since they have different surnames they're not even related. This greatly offends the German sense of order (see page 6).

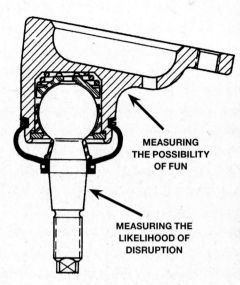

MEASURING THE POSSIBILITY OF FUN

MEASURING THE LIKELIHOOD OF DISRUPTION

FIG 8•5 **MECHANISM FOR GAUGING POSSIBLE BREAKS WITH TRADITION**

Humour

The German sense of humour is not invisible, as unkind cynics have suggested. It is different and specific. Germans don't find slapstick or silly things funny: their humour is more ironic and cynical, especially when aimed at the state of the world.

Q: How many Germans does it take to change a light bulb?

A: One. We are very efficient and this is not a joke.

The horn

The gender balance is more, er, balanced in Germany than many other countries.

German men

German men have a reputation for being rather backwards in coming forwards, often living with their parents well into their twenties and preferring beer and football (this is, in fairness, not specifically a German problem).

German women

German women are known as intelligent and assertive, and are unlikely to respond to chat-up lines such as:

i) Leute nennen mich Steve, aber Sie können mich anrufen heute Abend. (People call me Steve, but you can call me tonight.)

ii) Ich bin kein Mathematiker, aber ich bin ziemlich gut mit Zahlen. Ich sag dir was, Geben Sie mir Ihre und sehen, was ich damit machen kann. (I'm no mathematician, but I'm pretty good with numbers. Tell you what: give me yours and watch what I can do with it.)

Actually, that's not quite true: German women will respond by looking at you like something malodorously canine which they've just found on their shoe.

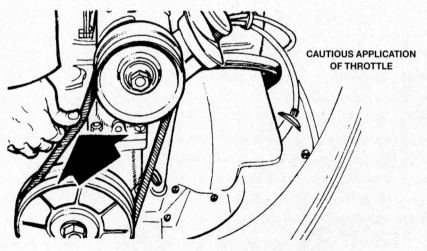

CAUTIOUS APPLICATION OF THROTTLE

FIG 8•6 **REVVING UP, GERMAN-STYLE. SLOWLY**

⚠ Germans and sex (umpapa)

When the Germans do finally get round to sex they're very frank in discussing it, and if you're embarrassed, they reckon that says more about you than anything bedroom-related you might admit to. German sex is not a matter of smouldering seduction like the French, or operatic crescendo like the Italians. German sex is more like a vigorous workout after which you can shower, fill in a feedback form with ratings and suggestions, shake hands and bid each other auf wiedersehen.

They also have a storied history of sex on camera, mainly involving extravagantly moustachioed men from the 1970s who've come to clean your pool/be your new tennis coach/ fix your washing machine, whose every movement is soundtracked by a wah-wah guitar, and whose vocabulary is limited to the phrases 'schnell schnell' and 'ich komme'.

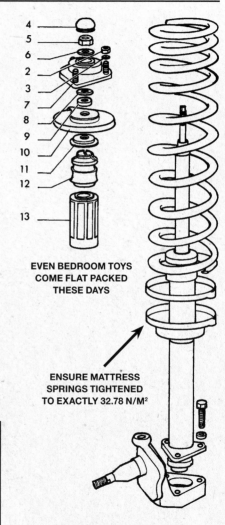

EVEN BEDROOM TOYS COME FLAT PACKED THESE DAYS

ENSURE MATTRESS SPRINGS TIGHTENED TO EXACTLY 32.78 N/M²

FIG 8•7 **ESSENTIAL PRE-SEX PREPARATIONS. NOT TO BE SKIPPED**

WARNING

Things have come a long way since the days when the role of women was defined as 'Kinder, Küche, Kirche' – children, kitchen, church.

Road manners

The Germans drive faster and better than any other nation in Europe. Their autobahnen are works of art, if your definition of art includes a minimum width of 3.75 metres, wide landscaped run-offs, double-sided guardrails, long acceleration and deceleration lanes, full grade separation, grades of 4% or less, well-banked curves and freeze-resistant concrete. (If that is your definition of art, you really are a German and this book has little to teach you.)

Not all the autobahn system is derestricted, but much of it is and if you drive on unlimited sections, remember one rule above all else – the left lane is for driving very, very fast indeed, and only for driving very, very fast indeed. If you're in the middle lane and pull out to overtake someone, make sure you can see no-one in your mirrors, not even a speck in the distance, as a speck in the distance closing at 250km/h will in a few seconds be a brake-hitting horn-blaring headlight-flashing outraged Audi driver right on your bumper.

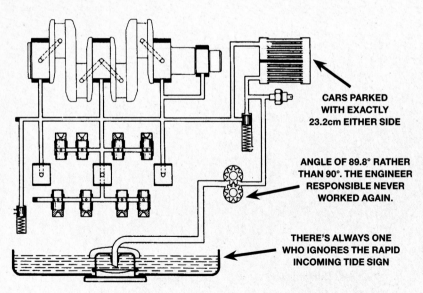

CARS PARKED
WITH EXACTLY
23.2cm EITHER SIDE

ANGLE OF 89.8° RATHER
THAN 90°. THE ENGINEER
RESPONSIBLE NEVER
WORKED AGAIN.

THERE'S ALWAYS ONE
WHO IGNORES THE RAPID
INCOMING TIDE SIGN

FIG 8•8 **PRINCIPLES OF GERMAN TRAFFIC MANAGEMENT**

⚠ Pedestrians

The quickest way to send the locals into meltdown is to cross a road against a red light. Doesn't matter if it's 2am, doesn't matter if there are no cars around, doesn't matter if the apocalypse has come and the oilfields have run dry and no vehicle has moved anywhere in the world for 20 years – the Germans, irrespective of age, colour or creed, will still wait patiently by the roadside until the little red man becomes the little green man and they're allowed to cross. To the Germans, therefore, pretty much every other country's pedestrian behaviour is like an outtake from Grand Theft Auto.

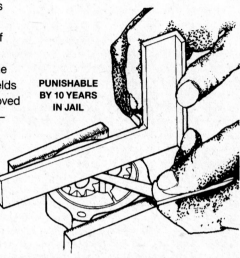

PUNISHABLE BY 10 YEARS IN JAIL

FIG 8•9 **TRYING TO FIX THE SYSTEM TO MAKE THE GREEN MAN APPEAR QUICKER**

Essential DOs and DON'Ts

✓ **DO** walk in a straight line when crossing. Zigzagging = not in Ordnung.

✓ **DO** proceed at a brisk but manageable pace. Everyone else will be.

✓ **DO** wear as much hi-vis gear as possible. Think railway worker and go upwards.

✗ **DON'T** smile at people coming the other way. It'll put them off their stride.

✗ **DON'T** look at your phone while crossing. It reduces briskness and increases zigzagging.

✗ **DON'T** play chicken with the three-second countdown. The moment the drivers see a green light, it's like the start at Silverstone.

Vehicle interior

The Germans see themselves as simple, honest folk who pay their bills on time and yet still feel the weight of the world on their shoulders. They're full of angst, Weltschmerz and Sturm und Drang. (They're also full of currywurst and pils.)

Since the end of World War Two, and with the spectre of Nazism casting a gigantic psychic shadow on the nation, the Germans have explicitly conflated their own identity with that of Europe. They're the heart of Europe in every way – geographically, politically, economically, financially – and regard being European as both intrinsically German and also an escape from being German.

This is one of the reasons why the European crisis so vexes the Germans. This, and the following joke: A Greek, a Portuguese, a Spaniard and an Irishman go into a bar. Who pays? The German. Of course, nowhere is Germany's place in Europe more important than when it comes to Austria next door. Luckily, some 80% of Austrians are happy with their neighbours. 100% of Austrians would like the rest of the world to know they are a separate country.

The word 'gymnasium' in German refers to a school rather than an indoor exercise facility. German gymnasiums do not therefore oblige you to pay extortionate monthly fees and/or attend three times a week in January and never thereafter.

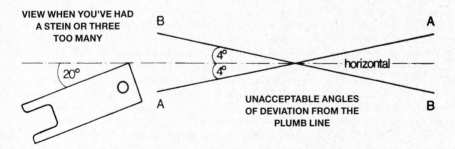

VIEW WHEN YOU'VE HAD A STEIN OR THREE TOO MANY

B

A

20°

4°

4°

horizontal

O

A

UNACCEPTABLE ANGLES OF DEVIATION FROM THE PLUMB LINE

B

FIG 8•10 **GERMAN SELF-ANALYSIS SPIRIT LEVEL**

⚠ Will the German laugh?

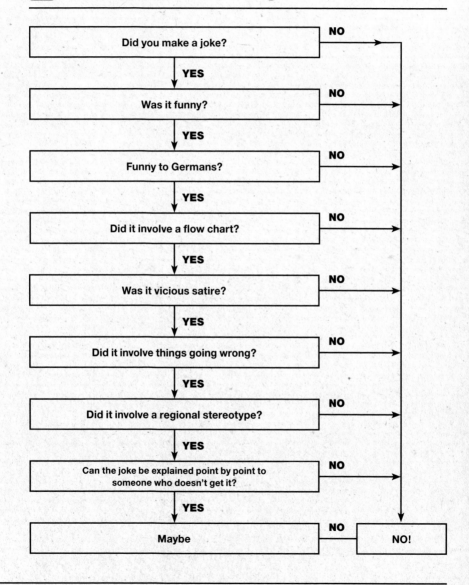

Vehicle exterior

How the Germans see the British

The Germans are puzzled by the British obsession with them in general and anything which happened before 1967 in particular, because the Germans in general like and admire the British.

They like British music: many middle-aged Germans grew up with and learnt English from Beatles records. They like British pomp and

ICH WETTE ER TRINKT CARLING BLACK LABEL

FIG 8•11 **ANGLO-GERMAN DRINKING APPARATUS**

circumstance, such as royal jubilees: sure, it might all be just for show, but mein Gott the Brits do it well.

They like the fact that the Brits are the only western Europeans who consistently get more drunk than they do. (Obviously eastern and northern Europeans are a whole different kettle of fish: beer may be the staple of the German and British drinker, but your average Russian or Finn doesn't even think of beer as alcohol, not when they have vodka/moonshine/brake fluid to hand.)

There are of course certain things which bemuse them. They think that putting vinegar on chips is the work of Satan himself. They shake their heads in exasperation at separate hot and cold taps. They have no idea how rail fares are calculated and regard the very concept of a 'super off peak' as something even Einstein (see 'famous models') would have struggled with.

Older Germans still have the idea that the British are elegant and polite, wear bowler hats and pinstripes, take tea and cucumber sandwiches at exactly 4pm, and live in stately homes with elderly retainers and a thriving class system. There is considerable crossover between the Germans who think this way and those who watch *Downton Abbey*.

How the Germans see the French

The Germans admire the French people's sophistication and concede that they are more cheerful and enjoy better weather (the Germans of course see the two as linked). They think Paris is beautiful, they love French fashion and they are rather in awe (though they will never admit it) of French food. The Germans have a phrase 'Leben wie Gott in Frankreich' – living like God in France – to describe a life of luxury.

Of course, they also see the French as standing with them at the centre of the European project – geographically, politically and economically. The historical enmity between the two countries has been replaced by a special relationship which is best seen through close personal relationships between the countries' leaders and suddenly stopping talking when the British enter the room because they weren't just gossiping about the Brits no they really weren't honest guv.

How the Germans see the Americans

The Germans admire the Americans for many things. They love their ambition, their optimism, their innovation and their generosity. They admire America's unabashed patriotism, but they also hope that America knows where it's going with it, as the Germans more than anyone know the dangers of jingoism.

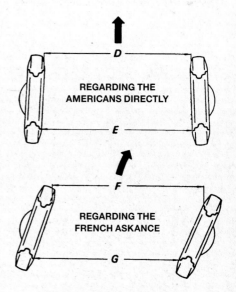

FIG 8·12 **LOOKING OUTWARDS: VARIABLE ANGLE MECHANISM**

The things they find strange about America are the things most Europeans find strange, such as the importance placed on religion, the healthcare system, the primacy of individual rights and the national obsession with firearms. German-Americans account for almost one-sixth of the US population and for one-third of ethnic Germans worldwide. Five American presidents have German ancestry, including those whose original surnames were Huber, Eisenhauer and Drumpf. No prizes for guessing – well, any of those, especially the last one.

Emission controls

The Germans are very environmentally conscious. Everywhere you go, you see colour-coded bins – recycling versions of the Teletubbies, more or less – into which you must put your refuse. Woe betide you if you refuse to put your refuse there or put the wrong item in the wrong bin. These are transgressions up there with crossing against a red light and incorrect gnome usage. Luckily, Haynes Explains is on hand to make sure you don't end up as the bin Laden of laden bins.

YOU'RE IN THE WRONG PLACE, MATE. TRY PAGE 30

FIG 8•13 **A GROUNDSMAN'S LINE-MARKING MACHINE**

1. Blue
All paper, cardboard, newspapers, magazines etc. goes in here. But not tissues. Fear not. We'll get to the tissue issue in good time.

2. Yellow
Cans, plastic, polystyrene etc. Do NOT put items inside each other: a yoghurt pot inside a baked beans tin represents alles very much not in Ordnung. You know why? Because at the other end this gets sorted by hand. Maybe by a bloke called Hans who's heard all the 'Hans hands' jokes and doesn't find them in any way funny any more, especially since you didn't rinse any of your containers before putting them in the bin.

3. Brown
Biological waste – kitchen scraps, peels, leftover food, coffee filters, tea bags, etc. In the summer months you can always tell where the brown bin is without needing to look.

4. Grey
Normal household waste not covered above. INCLUDING TISSUES! Don't forget the tissues. All this stuff goes for incineration, so don't put any of that pesky hazardous waste stuff (batteries, aerosols etc) in there.

Glass

Glass goes into the designated municipal bins, though only within certain hours. If you wake up in the middle of the night and want to know the time, simply go to the nearest bottle bank and start putting your empty bottles in. At the first tinkling of glass you'll have two dozen people yelling 'Bist du verrückt? Es ist drei uhr!', and you'll know (a) it's 3 a.m. (b) they think you're insane. You can even have similar fun during normal daylight hours, as all glass bins have separate slots for clear, green and brown glass. Failing to match bottle with slot will also have the locals shouting at you (in the brief moment before your assault on their sense of Ordnung causes them to malfunction like HAL in 2001).

Recycling

A man from Cologne was jailed for modifying a bottle recycling machine so it paid out €44,362.75 (the Germans like to be precise, as you may have guessed by now) without recycling a single bottle. Using a magnet sensor and a makeshift wooden tunnel, he managed to trick the machine into thinking that he was putting a new bottle in every time when in fact all he was doing was using the same one over and over again. 177,451 times. 'I had a radio next to it because otherwise it was really boring' said our hero before beginning his time in chokey.

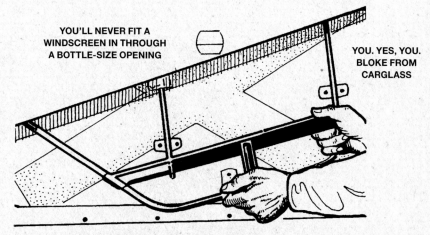

YOU'LL NEVER FIT A WINDSCREEN IN THROUGH A BOTTLE-SIZE OPENING

YOU. YES, YOU. BLOKE FROM CARGLASS

FIG 8•14 **PERSONS PROHIBITED FROM MUNICIPAL GLASS RECYCLING CENTRES**

Car financing

All you need to know about the German attitude to money is that their word for debt – Schuld – is the same as their word for guilt. The scars left by hyperinflation in the 1920s, when $1 went from being worth 4 DM to being worth 4,000,000,000,000 DM, run deep. (This of course also helps explain why they were so hacked off at being asked to repeatedly bail Greece out. As far as the Germans are concerned, when Greece is the word then it's Germany who's got bills and they're multiplyyyyyyyying.)

Insurance

Unsurprisingly, Germany is a land of insurance. Just as if you can name it so you can join a club for it, so too can you be insured against it. Life insurance, health insurance, household insurance, car insurance, travel insurance, bicycle insurance, unemployment insurance, salary insurance, pension insurance, kidnap insurance, ransom insurance, kidnap and ransom insurance, insurance scam insurance…. and we've only just uncovered the tip of the iceberg. (You can almost certainly get insurance against icebergs too if you know where to look, though in fairness there's only so much harm a lettuce can do.)

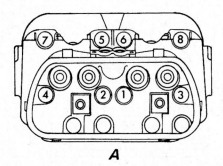

A

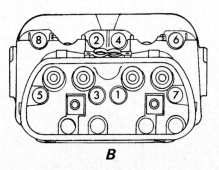

B

FIG 8•15 **SPECIAL GERMAN BOX FOR PARKING METER CHANGE, SEPARATED BY COIN DENOMINATION**

Most Germans have so many insurance policies that they need to build a special extension to house all the paperwork.

Doing business with Germans

a) The Germans like to concentrate on the task at hand. Come on. You can't pretend this surprises you, does it? Whereas the French, for example, like to get to know you a bit before doing business, the Germans are the other way round. They care if you can do business together, not if you like each other.

b) The German corporate structure doesn't exactly lend itself to freewheeling decisions made on the hoof. There are rules and regulations, procedures and processes. The Germans love all this, of course. Phrases you will never hear – 'let's sort out the details later.' Nein, mein Herr. No-one's leaving this room till every last detail's sorted out. Oh, you need the bathroom, do you? Let's agree on the exact number of paperclips covered by this deal, and THEN you can go. Maybe.

c) Be on time (see 'punctuality'). Being shambolic like Hugh Grant at the start of *Four Weddings* is not a good business look. Sauntering in half an hour late as though this is Spain is not a good look. The meeting will start without you if you're late.

d) You can work all week with a German and then have him show not the slightest interest in what you're doing all weekend, let alone invite you round. This does not necessarily mean he doesn't like you. It just means that he likes to keep his work and private life separate. If you're there for six months and he still hasn't asked you round, however, it's probably that he doesn't like you. Which is not surprising, let's face it. Look at the state of you.

e) The Germans will not hide behind management-speak. They will tell you clearly and bluntly what they think of your proposals. But even if you put forward a plan which is clearly risible, they will not laugh. The boss man may curl his lip to an angle of 18.7° to indicate his low opinion of your plan, but he will not laugh. Because the Germans are so direct, they often miss the more subtle non-verbal communication cues which other nationalities like to use. Rest assured, however, that even the Germans recognise the meaning of the lightly clenched fist moved back and forth to signal that your interlocutor is no stranger to onanism.

Model history

AD 410

The Visigoths sack Rome. Long before that, the Goths were an undisciplined rabble and the Romans the acme of military power and organisation. Yes – the Germans originally learnt order from the Italians. Things You Literally Could Not Have Made Up #732893.

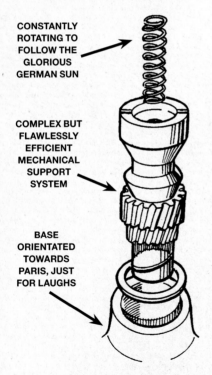

CONSTANTLY ROTATING TO FOLLOW THE GLORIOUS GERMAN SUN

COMPLEX BUT FLAWLESSLY EFFICIENT MECHANICAL SUPPORT SYSTEM

BASE ORIENTATED TOWARDS PARIS, JUST FOR LAUGHS

FIG 8•16 **BUILDING A VICTORY STATUE, GERMAN-STYLE**

Leader of said Visigoths (not to be confused with the Ostrogoths) was Alaric, who had to deal with 12 competing tribes led by his arch-rivals:

1) Chivalric. The most polite of all. Always ushering others forward.
2) Citric. Didn't do much: just stood around like a lemon.
3) Concentric. Rumoured to have invented crop circles.
4) Gastric. Disabled his opponents by serving uncooked food.
5) Geriatric. Old, wily and experienced campaigner.
6) Hydroelectric. Lived on the Rhine. A bright spark.
7) Mesmeric. Keen on hypnotising his opponents.
8) Obstetric. Excellent youth policy.
9) Podiatric. Best marchers of all due to their excellent footcare regime.
10) Psychiatric. Spent most of his time on a couch.
11) Theatric. Good at inspiring his troops with stirring speeches.
12) Vampiric. Only came out at night.

It was of course Vampiric who eventually triumphed, which is why Goths nowadays have black hair, black eyeliner, black fingernails, black clothes, and listen to music which even Joy Division would have thought too depressing.

1517

Martin Luther nails his 95 Theses to the door of All Saints' Church in Wittenberg, and only after doing so thinks of five more which would have made a nice round number. On the positive side, he stands firm against contemporary obsessions with witchcraft when recording his seminal track, I Got 95 Theses (And A Witch Ain't One). Luther is well known to British schoolchildren for existing on a diet of worms. The disappointment said children feel when told that the Diet of Worms was a legislative assembly is a contributory factor in declining numbers of history students. In later years, the ghost of Luther was reported to have been 'really annoyed' that he hadn't thought of the 'I have a dream' line first.

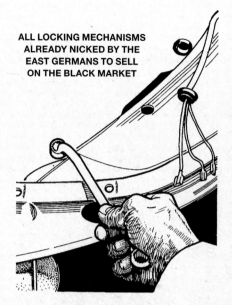

ALL LOCKING MECHANISMS ALREADY NICKED BY THE EAST GERMANS TO SELL ON THE BLACK MARKET

FIG 8•17 **FRUITLESS ATTEMPTS TO CLOSE THE BERLIN WALL, 9 NOVEMBER 1989**

1871

Germany is unified after Lord Palmerston declares the Schleswig-Holstein question to be no longer an issue, explaining 'it's so complicated that only three men in Europe have ever understood it. One was Prince Albert, who's dead. The second was a German professor who became mad. I'm the third and I've forgotten it.' Kaiser Wilhelm is proclaimed emperor in the Hall of Mirrors at Versailles, a holiday destination the Germans so enjoy that they return there in 1914 and 1940.

1949

Germany splits into East and West. The West gets money and democracy. The East gets all the best jokes. Why do Stasi officers make such good taxi drivers? You get in the car and they already know your name and where you live.

This division persists until 1989, when the Berlin Wall comes down and West Berlin hosts the largest ever single-day influx of stonewashed jeans and mullet haircuts ever recorded.

Famous models

Johannes Gutenberg (1398-1468)
Inventor of movable type, widely considered the greatest invention since the wheel and only superseded since by sliced bread, the telephone and those hard hats with straws attached so you can drink beer without using your hands. Before Gutenberg came along, it took one scribe a year to write out an entire illustrated Bible, and often much longer depending on how quickly he realised he'd spelt 'Deuteronomy' wrong.

There were only 30,000 books in Europe pre-Gutenberg: in the next century and a half the technology expanded so fast that 200 million books were printed, which in turn played a key role in bringing knowledge to the masses and driving the Renaissance, the Reformation, the Age of Enlightenment, the scientific revolution and *Fifty Shades Of Grey*.

Not to be confused with: *Steve Guttenberg, star of Sharknado: the 4th Awakens, Police Academy 4: Citizens On Patrol and Single Santa Seeks Mrs. Claus.*

Gutenberg printed 180 Bibles, of which 49 are known to still exist. A hitherto undiscovered complete copy would fetch £25m at auction.

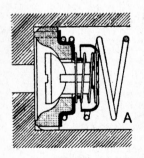

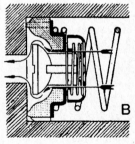

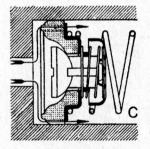

| TONER FADE | PAPER JAM | THE PRICE OF INK CARTRIDGES |

FIG 8•18 **PERENNIAL PRINTER PROBLEMS, 1450-PRESENT DAY**

Karl Marx (1818-1883)

Philosopher and thriller writer. His most riveting reads include *The Philosophical Manifesto of the Historical School of Law, Critique of Hegel's Philosophy of Right, Economic and Philosophic Manuscripts of 1844* (not as good as *Economic and Philosophic Manuscripts of 1843*, if you ask me, but hard for the lad to sustain that kind of form year-on-year), *A Contribution to the Critique of Political Economy* and *Theories of Surplus Value.*

Blamed capitalism for the ills of the world long before it was fashionable (there are those Germans being early for everything again). Confused everybody by announcing in 1880 'all I know is I'm not a Marxist.'

Not to be confused with: *Groucho, Chico, Harpo, Zeppo, Richard.*

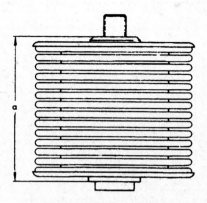

FIG 8•19 **CONVECTION CONDUCTORS DEMONSTRATING EINSTEIN'S PRETTY GIRL/STOVE THEORY**

Albert Einstein (1879-1955)

The man who came up with $E = mc^2$, the most famous equation in history. Heck, pretty much the only famous equation in history, let's face it.

Einstein's also famous for the theory of relativity, which in his own words goes something like this: when you're courting a nice girl an hour seems like a second, and when you're sitting on a burning stove a second seems like an hour.

Reassuringly cynical: 'two things are infinite, the universe and human stupidity, and I'm not sure about the universe.' His crazy hair and expressive face made him the template for the mad scientist archetype.

Not to be confused with: *Prince Albert, Albert Finney.*

WARNING

Do you subscribe to Marxist theories of economic redistribution and capitalist exploitation? Do you live in North London? Do you have a white beard? You do? Very glad to have you as a reader, Jezza.

Language selection

Millions of Germans speak English fluently, but deep down they consider it to be way too haphazard a language to be taken seriously. How can 'plough', 'through' and 'enough' rhyme when written but not when spoken? How can 'break' and 'steak' rhyme, and 'bleak' and 'streak', but not 'break' with 'bleak' or 'steak' with 'streak'? No: English is making it up as it goes along, and the Germans can't be doing with that. German is strictly logical. That's why it runs words together to make longer words, because if they belong together then they should be together. For the Germans, that Llanfair etc. train station name in Wales is amateur hour.

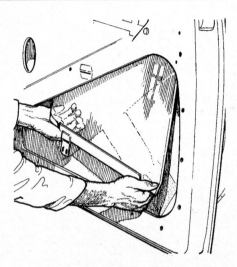

FIG 8•20 **ENSURING THAT GERMAN WORDS ARE THE CORRECT LENGTH**

Donaudampfschiffahrtselektrizitätenhauptbetriebswerkbauunterbeamtengesellschaft
Association of sub-ordinate officials of the head office management of the Danube steamboat electrical services.

Rindfleischetikettierungsüberwachungsaufgabenübertragungsgesetz
Beef labelling regulation and delegation of supervision law.

Betäubungsmittelverschreibungsverordnung
Regulation concerning the prescription of anaesthetics.

Vorstandsvergütungsangemessenheitsgesetz
Act for the appropriateness of the payment of a board of directors.

Hottentottenpotentatentantenattentat
An attempt on the life of the aunt of a Hottentot potentate.

Lost in translation

German	English
Schadenfreude	('damage joy'), which means 'pleasure in someone else's misfortune'.
Backpfeifengesicht	('slap face') Someone who is just crying out for, and would be greatly improved by, a damn good shoeing.
Drachenfutter	('dragon feed') A gift specifically intended and offered to placate someone angry at the giver. 99.99% of the time from a husband to his wife.
Erklärungsnot	('explanation poverty') When put on the spot, not to have a decent excuse either for something you should have done but haven't, or something you shouldn't have done but have.
Fachidiot	('subject idiot') Someone who knows everything about a specific field, the narrower and more obtuse the better, but nothing about anything else.
Handschuhschneeballwerfer	('someone who wears gloves to throw snowballs') A coward who criticises and abuses, but only from a safe distance and/or behind someone's back.
Kummerspeck	('grief bacon') The excess weight put on by overeating in response to emotional trauma. More usually ice-cream or chocolate rather than bacon, but the Germans do like their meat-based metaphors.
Pantoffelheld	('slipper hero') A man who acts tough in front of his friends but is totally under his wife's thumb.
Schnapsidee	('schnapps idea') An absolutely brilliant idea you had when drunk which in the cold and sober (well, cold and hungover) light of day makes substantially less sense.
Verschlimmbesserung	('worsening/improving') Of a situation, trying to make things better but actually making them worse.
Zugzwang	('compulsion to move') Originally a chess term meaning that any move you make will worsen your position, but also more generally of a situation: whatever you do, you're screwed.

Recreational vehicle

Think of the Germans on holiday and two words spring inexorably to mind – 'beach' and 'towels'. No matter how early you get up to reserve your sunlounger for the day, Horst and Helga will have beaten you to it. This is no accident. They will already have worked out all the essentials: optimal routes and waking times, sun direction and intensity, ease of access to the bar, and so on.

SEAL OFF BOTH THE ENTRANCE...

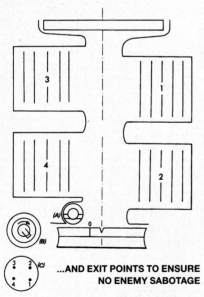

...AND EXIT POINTS TO ENSURE NO ENEMY SABOTAGE

FIG 8•21 **BEACH TOWELS: PLACEMENT TACTICS AND OPTIMAL LAYOUT**

Even when there are no sunloungers to be found, the Germans find a way of making the beaches their own. Their sandcastles boast concentrically arranged fortifications in frankly alarming detail, and areas are carved out for the playing of beach tennis and other healthy activities.

Of course, there's another thing which tends to happen at the confluence of Germans and beaches. More than a quarter of all Germans like a spot of nude sunbathing, and of course being German they have a name and organisation for it: the Freikörperkultur (FKK) movement, or Free Body Culture. As ever with these things, the ratio of people you would like to see unclothed to those who actually do get unclothed is as small and unimpressive as the average German male nudist's frankfurter after a dip in the North Sea.

The more like work the Germans can make their holidays, the more at home they feel. Leisure time is nothing if not an Opportunity For Self-Improvement.

⚠ The German menu

Did you hear about the vegetarian German pessimist? He feared the wurst. And with good reason: a typical German menu includes Bockwurst, Wiener Wurst, Blutwurst, Cervelatwurst, Bratwurst, Currywurst, Weißwurst, Brühwurst, Kinderwurst, Sommerwurst, Rostbratwurst, Mettwurst, Teewurst, Fleischwurst, Jagdwurst, Leberwurst....

It's possible, even likely, that you can spend months in Germany without anything green passing your lips. The idea that vegetables (other than the humble potato) can form part of a meal would come as a great and not entirely welcome surprise to many Germans.

'One cannot live from bread alone' they like to say. 'There must be sausage and ham as well.' They eat more pork than any other European country, and the well-upholstered German posterior may be the reason why Mercedes seats have traditionally been about as hard and unyielding as a church pew.

Beer

And of course all this meat must be washed down, and it must be washed down by beer. The Germans take their beer extremely seriously, to the extent that a Bavarian proverb makes a nutritional equation between three

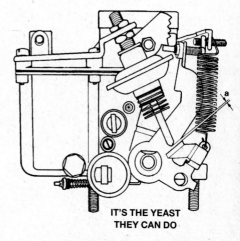

IT'S THE YEAST THEY CAN DO

FIG 8•22 **GERMAN BREWERY MACHINERY**

beers and a proper lunch. (They still have a proper lunch to go with the three beers, just in case). Germany has more than 5,000 different brands of beer and strict laws dating back 500 years about which ingredients may and may not be used.

When you think of German beer, you of course think of Oktoberfest. Enormous steins of beer? Check. Lederhosen and dirndl? Check. Oompah bands? Check. All German clichés present and correct, apart from one: with a lack of logic which is very unGerman, Oktoberfest actually begins in September.

Sportscars

'Football is a simple game. 22 men chase a ball for 90 minutes and at the end the Germans always win.'
– Gary Lineker

Football is the number one sport in Germany, not least because they're very good at it. They've won the World Cup four times, finished runners-up on another four occasions, and been semi-finalists five times. No other nation has reached the last four more often. Their clubs enjoy considerable success in European competition. Several clubs incorporate numbers in their names, including Darmstadt 98, TSG 1899 Hoffenheim, Schalke 04, Maroon 5 and 2468 Whodoweappreciate.

The least popular man in German football: the Borussia Mönchengladbach fan who always starts the 'give us a B' chant.

There's no way of measuring this properly, but the bullet header with which balding Bulgarian Yordan Letchkov knocked Germany out of the 1994 World Cup may have given more football fans in more countries more happiness than any other single moment.

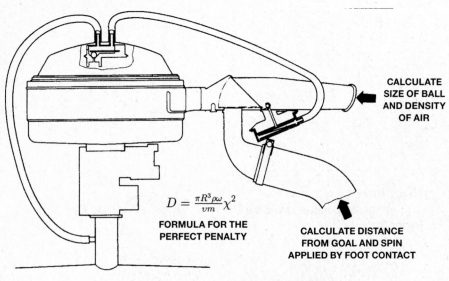

CALCULATE SIZE OF BALL AND DENSITY OF AIR

$$D = \frac{\pi R^3 \rho \omega}{vm} \chi^2$$

FORMULA FOR THE PERFECT PENALTY

CALCULATE DISTANCE FROM GOAL AND SPIN APPLIED BY FOOT CONTACT

FIG 8•23 **GERMAN PENALTY SHOOTOUT MACHINE**

Famous German footballers

Franz Beckenbauer

Elegant defender and talismanic captain nicknamed Der Kaiser, which is about as German a nickname as you can get. Once played against Italy with a dislocated shoulder and his arm in a sling. Finished his career with the New York Cosmos, whose owner was unimpressed the first time he saw Beckenbauer play. 'I didn't pay a million bucks for a guy to hang around in defence. Tell the Kraut to get his ass up front.'

Jurgen Klinsmann

Striker who whenever tackled acted as though he'd stepped on a land mine, throwing himself 200 feet in the air, rolling five times on impact, sneaking a quick peek at the referee, rolling five more times if no foul had been given, and then if still unsatisfied, leapt miraculously to his feet and appealed for a free kick in the manner of a Soviet prosecutor demanding the death penalty.

Oliver Kahn

The only goalkeeper ever to win the Golden Ball for the World Cup's best player. Tall, blond and so fearsome that his own defenders were more scared of him than the opposition were. Nicknamed Der Titan or Volcano. Facial expressions ran the gamut from malcontent to livid. Winner of 'Most German German' competition 1998–2003 inclusive. Not really a people person, according to teammate Bastian Schweinsteiger. 'In 2002 I joined Bayern Munich. My place in the dressing room was next to Kahn. The first time he talked to me was 2005.'

Kevin-Prince Boateng

Midfielder. Mainly for having the name 'Kevin-Prince.'

WHAT DO YOU MEAN, THEY GET NEW ONES FROM THEIR SPONSORS EACH GAME?

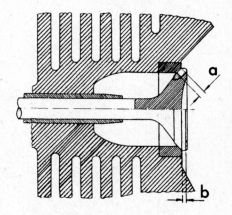

FIG 8·24 **GERMAN FOOTBALLER BOOT-SCRAPING SYSTEM**

In-car entertainment

German music is very much a game of two halves.

First half, tremendous play from the composers. Beethoven, even if by the end he was so deaf he thought he was a painter. Bach, still waiting for the biopic in which he's played by Arnie, because Arnie definitely said 'I'll be Bach.' Wagner and his Ring Cycle, which most people need a vindaloo to help achieve.

The second half was a totally different kettle of fish, Des. Let's look at the key moments.

1. Boney M
Big call to describe Ra-ra-Rasputin as Russia's greatest love machine. Also, the words 'it was a shame how he carried on' smack of judgmentalism.

2. Kraftwerk
Musically groundbreaking, sure. But those lecterns make them look like candidates in a presidential debate. And you could get your tailors to let your suits out a bit, boys. You haven't got the same size waist you did when you first fahrn fahrn fahrn auf der autobahn.

3. Nena
Sent a million teenage boys' hearts a-flutter until the moment she lifted up her arms. Someone get the woman a Ladyshave, quick!

4. Alphaville
You may very well be Big In Japan. But the 'skintight high-waisted jeans with dolman snow leopard top tucked in' look has never been Big Anywhere.

5. Rammstein
Teutonic loons. Live shows include walls of fire, operatic vocals, grinding thrash-metal/industrial guitars and lots of stuff you wouldn't show to your kids. Actually rather brilliant if you like that kind of thing.

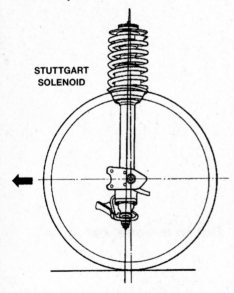

STUTTGART
SOLENOID

FIG 8•25 **TEUTONIC TURNTABLE**

⚠ Hollywood's take on soldiers

Hollywood World War Two movies have their own set of rules regarding the portrayal of German soldiers. These rules are (a) unbreakable (b) not necessarily historically accurate.

a) Of any two officers, one must be a die-hard Nazi and the other a reluctant servant of the Fatherland.

b) During any scene in which soldiers are taking cover, coming to battlestations or otherwise obliged to hurry, an officer must shout 'Schnell! Schnell!'

c) German officers must love opera and classical music.

d) German officers must have visited Paris before the war, and must look momentarily wistful when recalling the city's beauty.

e) All Nazi officers have a direct line to Heinrich Himmler in Berlin.

f) When talking to a superior, all Nazi officers will say only the words 'yes' or 'no' followed by the superior's rank. 'Ja, Standartenführer... Nein, Standartenführer.'

g) All German soldiers are exactly the same size as Allied soldiers, to enable a seamless swapping of uniforms for disguise purposes when either side is captured.

h) If a German actor is not available to play a German officer, a British actor with a cod-German accent will do fine.

i) For a movie set in occupied France, a pretty French girl bicycling past a café frequented by German soldiers is either about to open fire on them or acting as diversion for the attackers idling in a car around the corner.

World War II movies play fast and loose with history, no matter who makes them or which side they're on. Some are more realistic than others. But to anyone watching U-571, rest assured that in real life the Enigma machine was not stolen by Jon Bon Jovi.

Fault diagnosis

Fault	Diagnosis	Treatment
Is two minutes late	Cannot be German	Does not compute. Run error.
Crosses against red light	Cannot be German	Does not compute. Run error.
Voluntarily eats vegetables	Cannot be German	Does not compute. Run error.
Is not member of a club	Cannot be German	Does not compute. Run error.
Has never had mullet hair	Cannot be German	Does not compute. Run error.
Is amenable to other views	Cannot be German	Does not compute. Run error.
Makes recycling mistakes	Cannot be German	Does not compute. Run error.
Has fewer than 673 insurance policies	Cannot be German	Does not compute. Run error.
Rises after 5.30 a.m. on holiday	Cannot be German	Does not compute. Run error.
Loses to England at football	Cannot be German	Does not compute. Run error.

Conclusion

Mocking the Germans is a British national pastime. And there's plenty to mock. Apart from, well, the previous 30 or so pages, there's also the fact that you're most likely to come across the Germans on holiday, where some of them will almost certainly be complaining in an effort to secure a refund, a discount, or simply to pass the time. Their bible in such endeavours is the 'Frankfurt Table', which lists the percentage that may be reimbursed for specified shortcomings in tourism and travel services, and the Holy Grail is to claim back so much that they're actually being paid to go on holiday rather than vice versa.

In fairness, only a small proportion of Germans do that, and most of them are actually rather good as far as fellow holidaymakers go (often rather better than the Brits themselves, whisper it quietly). The Germans are very active on holiday, be it playing endless beach tennis or venturing further afield for activity holidays. Cyclists, for example, sport identical outfits and equipment, and hail you in perfect synchronicity as they pass, and you can always tell a German hiker not just by the poles they carry but by the fact they use them properly (as opposed to the British, who soon get bored of them and start swishing them around as though they were cricket bats, tennis racquets or fencing swords.) That the Germans are very into exercise is no surprise, since they're obsessed with their health to the point of hypochondria. There are few conditions deemed sufficiently benign not to merit a trip to the pharmacy or an extended sojourn in a spa resort.

But there's also an awful lot to admire in the Germans. Obviously not much of it has gone in here as it wouldn't be so much fun to be nice about them, but in no particular order there's their work ethic, their lack of hypocrisy, their interest in other countries and the wider world, the fact that millions of them speak better English than millions of us do, their automotive industry, their beautiful country, the fact that Berlin is probably the coolest of all European capitals, and so on.

If only they'd let us win a penalty shootout. Just one. Is that too much to ask?

Titles in the Haynes Explains series

Now that Haynes has explained Germans, you can progress to our full size manuals on car maintenance (efficiency personified), *Beer Manual* (fill up your Stein), *Home-Grown Vegetable Manual* (cabbage for your Sauerkraut), *Brass Instrument Manual* (start your own Oompah Band).

There are Haynes manuals on just about everything – but let us know if we've missed one.

Haynes.com